ACOUSTIC GUITAR PRIMER
Revised
by
BERT CASEY

INTRODUCTION

The *Acoustic Guitar Primer* with audio CD will quickly transform you from an absolute beginner into a student/guitarist with a full understanding of the fundamentals and techniques of guitar playing. This clear, step by step method includes many photographs, large easy to read notation and tablature, and a sequence of learning that has been meticulously developed and tested over a 25 year period. With each new song, you will learn new techniques to establish a firm foundation that will enable you to enjoy playing guitar for many years. No wonder the *Acoustic Guitar Primer* is the first choice of over 2,000 stores throughout the United States and Canada.

THE AUTHOR

Bert Casey, the author of this book, has been a professional performer and teacher in the Atlanta area for over 30 years. He plays several instruments (acoustic guitar, electric guitar, bass guitar, mandolin, banjo, and flute) and has written 7 other books (*Acoustic Guitar Book 2, Electric Guitar Primer, Bass Guitar Primer, Mandolin Primer, Ukulele Primer, Flatpicking Guitar Songs,* and *Bluegrass Fakebook*) and has made five DVDs/videos (*Introduction to Acoustic Guitar, Acoustic Guitar Part 2, Introduction to Electric Guitar, Introduction to Bass Guitar,* and *Introduction to Mandolin*). Bert performed many years in Atlanta and the Southeast with his bands Home Remedy and Blue Moon. His talent and willingness to share have helped thousands of students learn and experience the joy of playing a musical instrument.

WATCH & LEARN PRODUCTS REALLY WORK

30 years ago, Watch & Learn revolutionized music instructional courses by developing well thought out, step by step instructional methods that were tested for effectiveness on beginners before publication. These products, which have dramatically improved the understanding and success of beginning students, have evolved into Watch & Learn products that continue to set the standard of music instruction today. This has resulted in sales of almost 2 million products since 1979. This easy to understand course will significantly increase your success and enjoyment while playing the guitar.

CD, DVD, AND VIDEO COUNTER

The CD, DVD, and video counters are included in this book to show where each lesson is located on the companion CD, DVD, or video. Use your remote control on the DVD or CD player to skip to the track you want. Check the counter number as it appears on screen in the video and then scan to the exact location on the video.

COMPANION PRODUCTS

Watch & Learn, Inc. has two companion products which most students find invaluable for working through this course:

The *Intro to Acoustic Guitar DVD* allows you to see all the movements of the left and right hand. It covers the material in the book utilizing the latest in video technology (split screen, on screen tablature, state of the art graphics, special effects, and animation) to add further emphasis and clarity for the student. DVD $9.95

The *Acoustic Guitar Jam CDs* is a two CD set that plays the first 18 songs in the *Acoustic Guitar Primer* at three speeds along with an acoustic band (guitar, bass, mandolin, and vocals). All of the verses are sung at each speed with harmony parts added where appropriate. Quickly develop the ability to jam with others. 2 CD Set $14.95

FOLLOWUP PRODUCTS

The follow up course, *Acoustic Guitar Book 2,* takes you to the next level of playing rhythm guitar by teaching a variety of rock & country strums, arpeggios, bar chords, and how to play along with other guitarists. The student plays and sings along with a full band on extended versions of 17 popular songs. Book $14.95 DVD $14.95

If you want to continue with bluegrass lead guitar, *Flatpicking Guitar Songs* book with CD teaches how to become a flatpicker. It includes exciting arrangements to popular songs and is written in both tablature and notation. There are several breaks for each song and each break is played slow (for practicing) and fast (for performing) on the audio CD. Book $14.95

These products are available at your local store or send a check including $5.00 shipping and handling to the address below:

Watch & Learn, Inc.
1882 Queens Way
Atlanta, GA 30341
800-416-7088

TABLE OF CONTENTS

<table>
<tr><td></td><td>Page</td><td></td><td></td><td> 2:15</td><td></td></tr>
</table>

SECTION III - LEAD PLAYING

These icons or counters indicate the following products:

The companion audio CD found inside the back cover of this book.

The companion DVD, *Intro to Acoustic Guitar*.

The companion video, *Intro to Acoustic Guitar*.

The companion practice CD set, *Acoustic Guitar Jam CDs*.

SECTION 1
GETTING STARTED

THE GUITAR

 2:15

We recommend that you use a steel string guitar for this course. It is important that your instrument is easy to play and is free from buzzes or rings. An inferior instrument is often a handicap that forces the student to develop improper technique and quickly lose enthusiasm.

To insure that you are starting correctly, take your guitar to a local music store, a reputable teacher, or a guitar repair shop, and have them give it a quick check. If you need to buy a guitar, it is usually safer to purchase your first instrument from a reputable music store, who will make sure that the instrument is adjusted properly and offer service after the sale. Learning to play the guitar is a fun filled and rewarding experience, particularly if you have the proper instrument to get started on.

The following diagram illustrates a steel string guitar, which we recommend for use with this course.

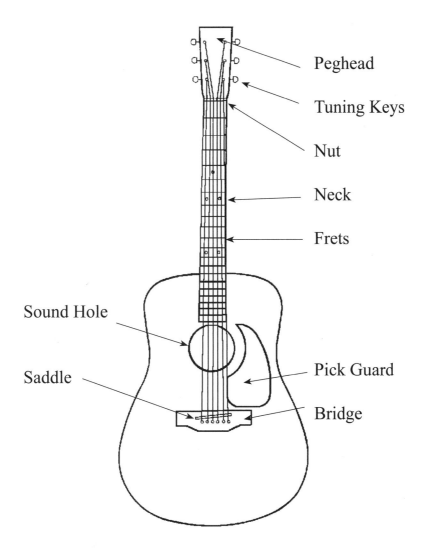

Peghead

Tuning Keys

Nut

Neck

Frets

Sound Hole

Pick Guard

Saddle

Bridge

 Get to know the folks at your local music store. They can be a great help with supplies, lessons, & advice.

1

HOLDING THE GUITAR

Many guitarists are self taught and have developed their own unique and sometimes unorthodox styles of holding and playing the guitar. We will be using the most common techniques that are approved and taught by instructors.

At first you will be holding the guitar sitting down. Use a straight back chair or stool so that you can sit with good posture and have free arm movement without banging the guitar or your arms on the furniture.

Sit erect with both feet on the floor and the guitar resting on your right thigh. The guitar should be braced against your chest with the right forearm so that the neck of the guitar doesn't move when you change hand positions.

This basic position allows both hands to move freely and allows your back to be comfortable during practice sessions.

TIP *Always use a case or gig bag when transporting your instrument from one place to another.*

TUNING THE GUITAR

Before playing the guitar, it must be tuned to standard pitch. If you have a piano at home, it can be used as a tuning source. The following picture shows which note on the piano to tune each open string of the guitar to.

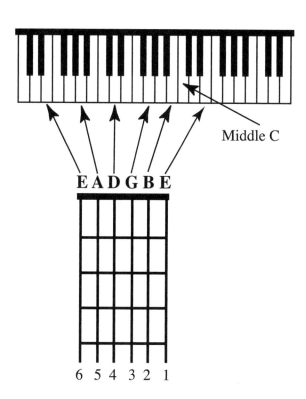

Middle C

E A D G B E

6 5 4 3 2 1

Note: If your piano hasn't been tuned recently, the guitar may not agree perfectly with a pitch pipe or tuning fork. Some older pianos are tuned a half step below standard pitch. In this case, use one of the following methods to tune.

PITCH PIPE

Pitch pipes are an easy and portable way of tuning a guitar. They may be obtained at a local music store with complete instructions.

CD OR DVD

It is recommended that you tune your guitar to the CD or DVD that accompanies this book so that you will be in tune when you play along with the songs and exercises.

ELECTRONIC TUNER

An electronic tuner is the fastest and most accurate way to tune a guitar. I highly recommend getting one. They are available for $20 - $50.

TIP *Never leave your instrument in a car or trunk during extreme heat or cold.*

RELATIVE TUNING

Relative tuning means to tune the guitar to itself and is used in the following situations:

1. When you do not have an electronic tuner or other source to tune from.
2. When you have only one note to tune from.

In the following example we will tune all of the strings to the 6th string of the guitar, which is an E note.

1. Place the ring finger of the left hand behind the fifth fret of the 6th string to fret the 1st note. Tune the 5th string open (not fretted) until it sounds like the 6th string fretted at the 5th fret.
2. Fret the 5th string at the 5th fret. Tune the 4th string open (not fretted) until it sounds like the 5th string at the 5th fret.
3. Fret the 4th string at the 5th fret. Tune the 3rd string open until it sounds like the 4th string at the 5th fret.
4. Fret the 3rd string at the 4th fret. Tune the 2nd string until it sounds like the 3rd string at the 4th fret.
5. Fret the 2nd string at the 5th fret. Tune the 1st string open until it sounds like the 2nd string at the 5th fret.

Now repeat the above procedure to fine tune the guitar. Until your ear develops, have your teacher or a guitar playing friend check the tuning to make sure it is correct.

The following diagram of the guitar fret board illustrates the above procedure.
Note - Old dull strings lose their tonal qualities and sometimes tune incorrectly.

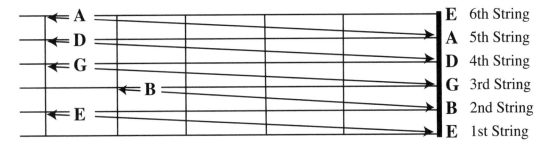

E	6th String
A	5th String
D	4th String
G	3rd String
B	2nd String
E	1st String

Check with your teacher or favorite music store to make sure your strings are in good playing condition.

THE PICK

SELECTING THE PICK

When you visit a music store, you will notice that there are almost as many pick styles and shapes as there are guitar players. A pick should feel comfortable in your hand and produce a clear, clean tone when picking or strumming the strings. This is the most popular pick shape.

HOLDING THE PICK

The grip on a pick should provide control while feeling comfortable. The most common way of holding the pick is to curl the right index finger (Figure 1), place the pick in the first joint of the index finger with the point facing straight out (Figure 2), and then place the thumb firmly on the pick with the thumb parallel to the first joint (Figure 3). Watch the DVD for further clarification.

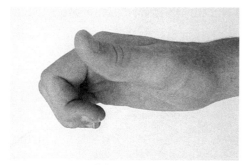

Figure 1

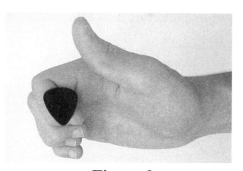

Figure 2

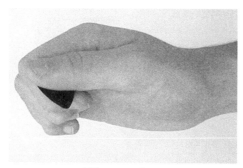

Figure 3

TIP

Keep many extra picks around. They like to disappear, much like socks.

RIGHT HAND POSITION

5:34

Position the right hand so that the pick strikes the strings between the bridge and the fretboard. The right forearm should be braced against the body of the guitar so that the right hand falls into a position towards the center of the sound hole. Too close to the bridge produces a harsh tone and too far forward produces a tone that is too mellow.

Too Harsh   **Correct**   **Too Mellow**

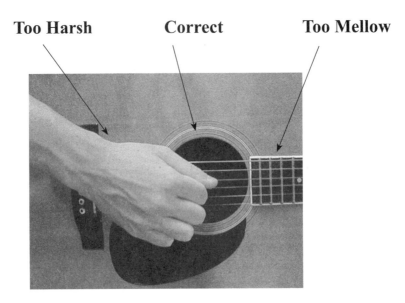

The right hand should be free with no part of the hand or wrist touching the guitar.

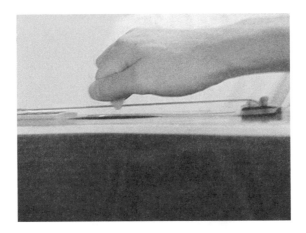

TIP *Use a guitar cloth to clean your guitar and wipe it down after you play.*

STRUMMING

 6:09

When you strum the guitar, start with the sixth string and lightly strum down on all six strings, stopping just past the first string.

Start Strum   **Finish Strum**

Don't use an exaggerated stroke that carries the right hand beyond the body of the guitar. Finish the strum according to the illustrations above.

Wasted Motion

Another common mistake is to bang down on the sixth string. Don't make any one string your point of attack. The correct way is to strum down lightly and evenly on all six strings so that it sounds like the DVD.

 **TIP** *Don't store your guitar in the attic or basement.*
Extreme dryness or dampness can be bad.

THUMB POSITION

When playing the guitar, the position of the left thumb on the back of the neck is very important because it is used to brace and balance the left hand. We're going to use what's called an elevated thumb placement.

ELEVATED THUMB PLACEMENT

The joint on the base of the left thumb is the brace point on the back of the guitar neck (Figure A). Place the base of the thumb on the center of the guitar neck (Figure B).

Figure A

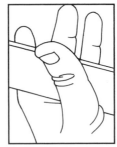

Figure B

OUR FIRST CHORD

We will now make a G chord as shown in the following diagrams:

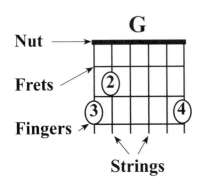

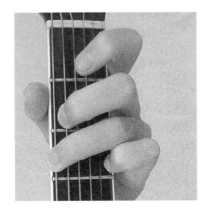

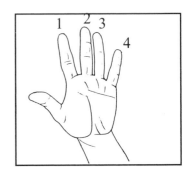

Check the following to make sure you are using good technique:

1. The bottom joint of the thumb should be placed on the center of the guitar neck (Figures A and B above).
2. The fingers should be arched so that the tips of the fingers fret the strings. Do not touch an adjacent string with one of your fingers. Check the following diagrams for the correct position.

8

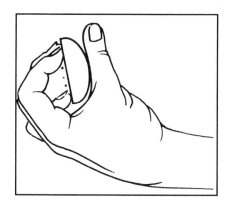
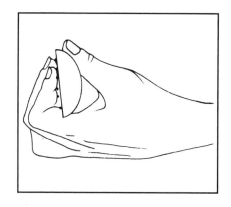

Correct - Fingers Arched   **Incorrect - Fingers Flat**

EXERCISE 1

Form the G Chord and strum the guitar from the 6th string down (towards the floor) in one smooth stroke. Do this several times while listening to the CD or DVD.

G - G - G - G - G - G - G - G - G - G - G - G - G - G - G - G

BUZZING, MUFFLED, & UNCLEAR NOTES

If you aren't getting a clear distinct sound when playing, check the following problem areas:

1. Not pressing hard enough with the left hand. Press the strings firmly but not so hard as to be painful. (We are assuming the guitar is properly adjusted).
2. Fingers too far from the fret wires or on top of the frets. The fingers of the left hand should be directly behind the frets. Check the diagrams on page 8.
3. Fingers touching an adjacent string. Make sure your fingers are arched properly.
4. Fingernails too long. Trim your fingernails so that the tips of the fingers can press down on the strings.
5. The guitar is not properly adjusted.

Note - Some method books use partial chords where only 3 or 4 strings are played because these are easier. In this book, we are using full chords because that is what is used in playing rhythm. Unfortunately, it sometimes takes 4 to 6 weeks for a beginner to be able to use these chords, so be patient. Your hand and finger muscles will strengthen and stretch, making it more comfortable to form the chords.

C CHORD

The C chord is another common chord. Position your fingers as shown:

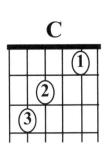

EXERCISE 2

Strum down lightly on the C chord towards the floor.. Do this until you get a consistently clear sound like you hear on the CD or DVD.

C - C - C - C - C - C - C - C - C - C - C - C - C - C - C - C

EXERCISE 3

Practice changing between the two chords you have learned so far. Strum once on the G chord, change to the C chord and strum once, go back to the G chord, etc.

G - C - G - C - G - C - G - C - G - C - G - C - G - C - G - C

Hint - Practice moving the left hand as one continuous movement. In this exercise concentrate on the middle and ring fingers. The index and little fingers will fall in place.

Note - If you have questions regarding chording the guitar, we recommend that you either purchase the DVD that accompanies this book or ask a qualified teacher.

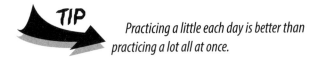

Practicing a little each day is better than practicing a lot all at once.

THE D CHORD

The third chord is a D chord. Position your fingers as shown:

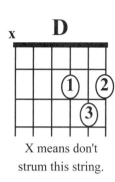

X means don't strum this string.

EXERCISE 4

Strum the D chord from the 4th string down towards the floor in one smooth stroke.

D - D - D - D - D - D - D - D - D - D - D - D - D - D - D - D

EXERCISE 5

Practice changing between the G & D chords, strumming once for each chord as follows:

G - D - G - D - G - D - G - D - G - D - G - D - G - D - G - D

EXERCISE 6

Now practice changing between all three chords.

G - C - D - G - C - D - G - C - D - G - C - D - G - C - D - G - C - D

Hint - One way to practice is to change from one chord to the other with the left hand only, without strumming with the right hand. When this feels comfortable, add the right hand strum.

TIP *Practice new songs slowly and relaxed. Work on speed after you can play it perfectly.*

11

PLAYING OUR FIRST SONG

Using the G, C, and D chords and a simple downstroke, we can now play our first songs. We'll start with songs that everybody knows. Every time you see the following mark (/), strum down one time. Play along with the CD or DVD.

TOM DOOLEY

Traditional

G

Hang	down	your head	Tom		Doo	-	ley	
/	/	/	/	/	/		/	/
1	2	3	4	1	2		3	4

                              D

Hang	down	your head	and		cry			
/	/	/	/	/	/	/	/	
1	2	3	4	1	2	3	4	

Hang	down	your head	Tom		Doo	-	ley	
/	/	/	/	/	/		/	/
1	2	3	4	1	2		3	4

                              G

Poor	boy	you're bound	to	die			
1	2	3	4	1	2	3	4
/	/	/	/	/	/	/	/

Kingston Trio - The Very Best of the Kingston Trio
Grateful Dead - Reckoning - Disc 2
Doc Watson - The Essential Doc Watson

12

Now we'll use the C & G chords to play another song. Count in the same manner and strum down on every beat. Again, play along with the CD or DVD.

HE'S GOT THE WHOLE WORLD 15:15 16-17

Traditional

He's got the

C

whole		world		in	his	hands	he's got the
/	/	/	/	/	/	/	/
1	2	3	4	1	2	3	4

G

whole		world		in	his	hands	he's got the
/	/	/	/	/	/	/	/
1	2	3	4	1	2	3	4

C

whole		world		in	his	hands	he's got the
/	/	/	/	/	/	/	/
1	2	3	4	1	2	3	4

G   **C**

whole	world	in	his	hands			
1	2	3	4	1	2	3	4
/	/	/	/	/	/	/	/

Next we'll use all three chords (G, C, & D) to play another song. Count in the same manner and play along with the CD or DVD.

GOING DOWN THAT ROAD... 16:58 18-19

Traditional

G

Going down			that	road		feeling		bad							
/	/	/	/	/	/	/	/	/	/	/	/	/	/	/	/
1	2	3	4	1	2	3	4	1	2	3	4	1	2	3	4

C   **G**

Going down			that	road		feeling		bad							
/	/	/	/	/	/	/	/	/	/	/	/	/	/	/	/
1	2	3	4	1	2	3	4	1	2	3	4	1	2	3	4

C   **G**

Going down			that	road		feeling		bad		Lord,		Lord,		and	I
/	/	/	/	/	/	/	/	/	/	/	/	/	/	/	/
1	2	3	4	1	2	3	4	1	2	3	4	1	2	3	4

D   **G**

ain't	gonna		be	treated		this	a	way							
/	/	/	/	/	/	/	/	/	/	/	/	/	/	/	/
1	2	3	4	1	2	3	4	1	2	3	4	1	2	3	4

TABLATURE

This book is written in both tablature and standard music notation. If you wish to learn to read music, consult your local music store for a good book or ask your music teacher for an explanation. We will explain tablature because it is easy to learn if you are teaching yourself and because a lot of popular guitar music is available in tablature.

Tablature is a system for writing music that shows the proper string and fret to play and which fingers to use. It also shows the proper pick direction. In guitar tablature, each line represents a string on the guitar. If the string is to be fretted, the fret number is written on the appropriate line. Otherwise a 0 is written. Study the examples below until you understand them thoroughly.

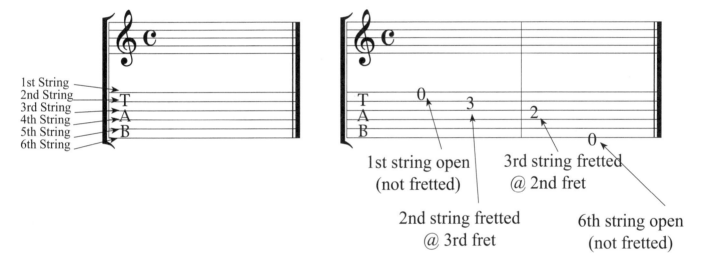

The music will be divided into either two sets of lines (staffs) or three sets of lines.

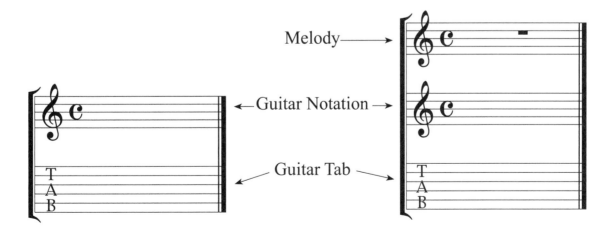

TIP — *Learning music theory will help you understand how music is written.*

At this point we'll start working on the G scale to help the coordination between the left and right hands. Most students will find scales easier than learning chords.

EXERCISE 9

Play the following scale exercise using all down strokes. The numbers in parenthesis indicate the left hand fingering.

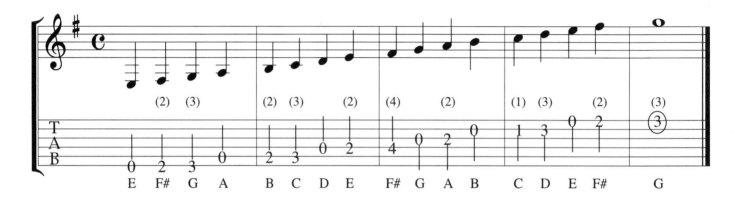

Notes:

1. Practice one string at a time, getting each note to sound clearly before moving on to the next string. Each note should be held an equal amount of time.

2. Use the same left hand finger as the fret you are playing. This is called "frets and fingers the same". For example:

   1st fret is played with the 1st finger of the left hand.
   2nd fret is played with the 2nd finger of the left hand.
   3rd fret is played with the 3rd finger of the left hand.
   4th fret is played with the 4th finger of the left hand.

3. Practice this exercise 5 minutes each day until you can play all of the notes.

4. The 1st and 2nd left hand fingers are much stronger than the 3rd and 4th fingers. It will take a few months of practice before the 3rd and 4th fingers gain strength.

 Working with a metronome helps you practice slowly and gradually increase speed.

 20:15

Play the reverse of Exercise 9 as follows:

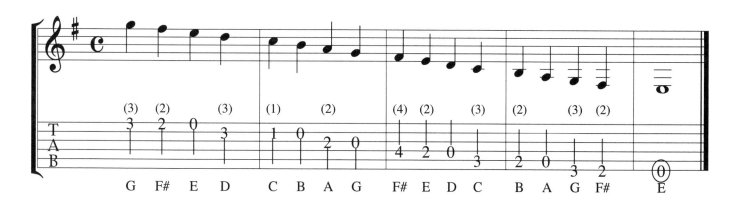

Practice the exercises until you can play them with no mistakes and have committed them to memory. At this point, close your eyes and continue practicing.

Each practice session should be divided between practicing chord changes, playing rhythm, and playing scales.

PRACTICE

The most important part of learning to play the guitar is to develop consistent and efficient practice habits. The beginning student must have patience because playing the guitar requires training the hands to do movements they have never done before and to strengthen muscles not normally used. You should average 30 minutes of practice each day. With consistent practice you should be comfortable with the guitar and be able to play a few songs within a couple of weeks. Once you learn to play a few things on the guitar, you'll find the learning process comes easier and your progress will start to snowball.

Following are some helpful hints and pointers concerning practice:

1. Practice 30 minutes a day if you are a beginner and 45 minutes if you are an intermediate. Divide this time into 15 or 20 minute segments.
2. Set up practice times to coincide with other activities such as when you wake up, when you go to bed, or when you come home at the end of the day. 10-15 minutes in the morning and 10-15 minutes at night works well for many people.
3. Go over your lesson assignment EVERY day. Even on days that it seems impossible to practice, make yourself go over the lesson for 4 or 5 minutes to reinforce things.
4. If possible, set up a special practice area. Buy an inexpensive music stand and keep your lessons on it so you can start to work immediately with each practice session.
5. Avoid marathon 2 or 3 hour practice sessions on the weekends. The mind can only concentrate for short periods and most marathon sessions accomplish about the same amount of learning as a 15 minute practice session. In addition, many students use the "Marathon Practice Session" as an excuse to not practice every day.
6. Learn to identify and focus on the hard parts of each song. Put your efforts there as opposed to playing a song from start to finish over and over. Some techniques and movements require several hundred repetitions over several weeks while others are learned immediately after a few tries.
7. Practice the guitar at first by looking in a mirror to make sure you are using the proper position.
8. Relax - if frustrated with a particular measure or technique, go to another or take a break and come back after you feel better.
9. Ask your teacher or a friend to let you know how you are doing every couple of weeks. It is very encouraging because they notice your progress even though you think you are standing still.
10. Record and listen to your own playing. This will help you locate areas that need work and also measure progress. Your tapes will improve as you practice more and more.
11. Remember always - Guitar playing is a lot of fun no matter what your level of competence. Relax and enjoy yourself.

BASS STRUM

At this point you should be fairly comfortable with the G, C, & D chords and be able to change between them while strumming. Now we'll add the bass string to the strum.

The simplest rhythm involves playing one of the bass strings and strumming down on the remaining strings.

EXERCISE 11

Form a G chord, pick the 6th string with a down stroke, then strum down on the G chord from the 5th string down through the 1st string, stopping the right hand just beyond the 1st string.

EXERCISE 12

1. Count from 1 to 4 out loud. Each number must be evenly spaced. You may pat your foot or use a metronome to make sure each number is even.

2. Form a G chord. Continue counting from 1 to 4. Play the 6th string by itself when you count 1 and 3. Strum on 2 and 4. Play along with the CD or DVD.

1	2	3	4	1	2	3	4
6th String	Strum	6th String	Strum	6th String	Strum	6th String	Strum

In tablature the exercise looks like this:

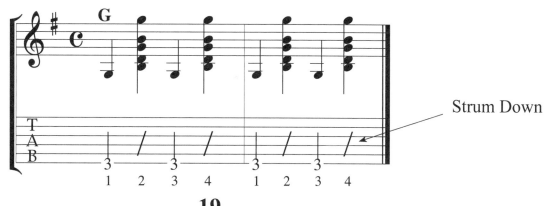

EXERCISE 13

Form a C chord, pick the 5th string, and strum from the 4th string down.

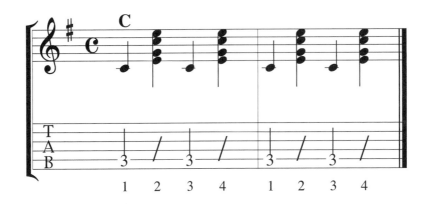

EXERCISE 14

Form a D chord, pick the 4th string, and strum from the 3rd string down.

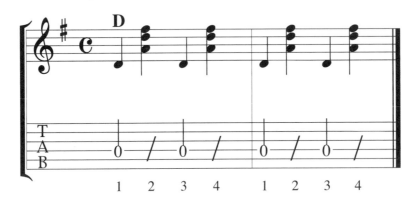

EXERCISE 15

Now combine all three chords into one exercise.

Repeat signs

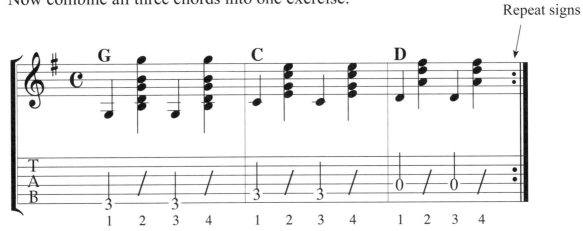

 *Try to find friends who play. Playing with others is great fun & you learn new things as well.*

20

This icon denotes the track numbers on the *Acoustic Guitar Practice CDs*. See page 29.

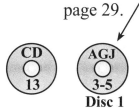

TOM DOOLEY

Traditional

 24:10

 23-24

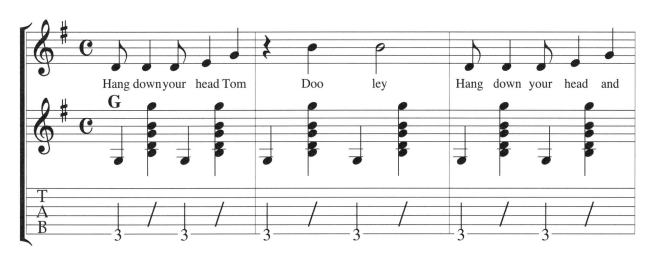

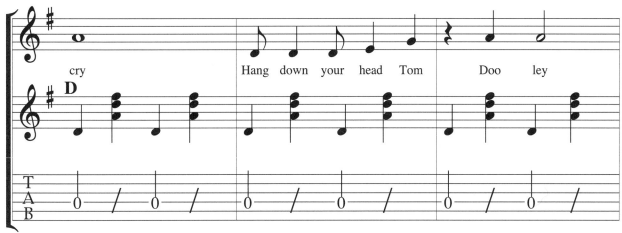

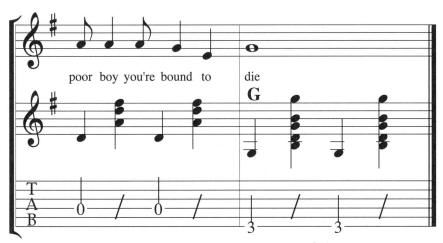

Kingston Trio - The Very Best of the Kingston Trio
Grateful Dead - Reckoning - Disc 2
Doc Watson - The Essential Doc Watson

21

GOING DOWN THAT ROAD

Go - ing down that road feel - ing bad

Go - ing down that road feel - ing bad

Go - ing down that road feel - ing bad Lord Lord And I

ain't gon - na be treat - ed this a way

22

Grateful Dead - 1973-06-10 RFK Stadium
Doc Watson - The Essential Doc Watson
Johnny Cash - The Survivors Live

ALTERNATING BASS RHYTHM

To put a little more variety in the strum, we'll alternate the bass notes. For instance with the G chord, instead of playing the 6th string over and over, we'll play the 6th string and strum, play the 4th string and strum from the 3rd string down. Remember to start the strum with the string next to and below the bass string.

EXERCISE 18

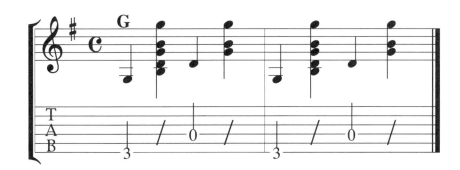

EXERCISE 19

Form a C chord and alternate between the 5th and 4th strings as follows:

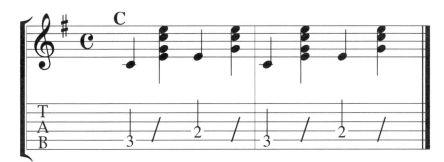

EXERCISE 20

Form a D chord and alternate between the 4th and 5th strings as follows:

 Purchase a music stand. People who use one tend to practice up to 30% longer.

23

Now practice using all three chords

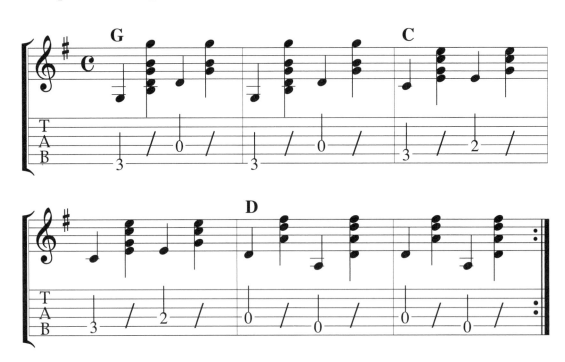

Note - Some people have difficulty getting a clear sound on the alternate bass notes because their fingers are too wide and touch adjacent strings or their fingers are too short and can't be arched properly. If you have this problem, you can compensate by:

1. Fretting the bass strings with the pad of the fingertip slightly towards the top side of the fretboard instead of squarely on the strings, i.e. on the G chord, move the middle finger slightly towards the 6th string instead of placing it squarely on the 5th string.

2. Lifting your finger off the primary bass note as you pick the alternate bass note, i.e. lift the ring finger off of the 5th string of the C chord when you pick the 4th string.

Now play the next song using the alternating bass rhythm. After you feel comfortable, play along with the CD or DVD.

HE'S GOT THE WHOLE WORLD 28:25
28-29

Traditional

25

WORRIED MAN BLUES

Johnny Cash - At Madison Square Gardens
Carter Family - Can The Circle Be Unbroken
Woody Guthrie - Pastures of Plenty

DOWN UP PICKING

Up to this point the right hand has played all the notes and strums using only down strokes. We will start mixing down strokes (towards the floor) with up strokes (towards the ceiling). Play the following exercise to develop your down up picking technique.

EXERCISE 24

Starting with the 6th string, play the 5th, 6th, 7th, and 8th frets using the index, middle, ring, and little fingers of the left hand. Play along with the CD or DVD.

CLASSICAL THUMB PLACEMENT

Notice that we use the classical placement of the thumb on the back of the neck to permit the fingers of the left hand to stretch more.

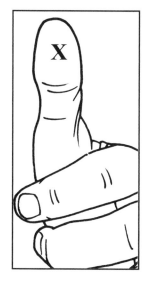 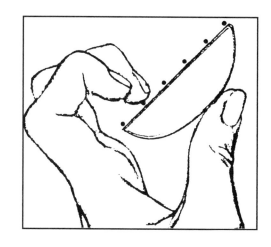

 Keep your instrument from being knocked over. Purchase a guitar stand.

EXERCISE 25

Continue on each string playing the 5th, 6th, 7th, and 8th frets using the alternating down and up strokes with the right hand. The complete exercise looks like this:

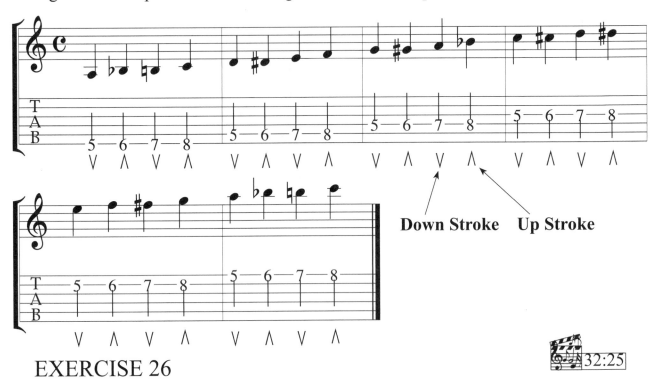

Down Stroke   Up Stroke

EXERCISE 26

Play the reverse of Exercise 25 by starting at the 1st string at the 8th fret and coming back down.

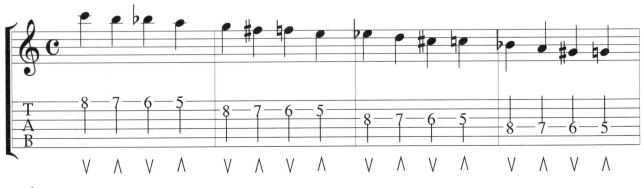

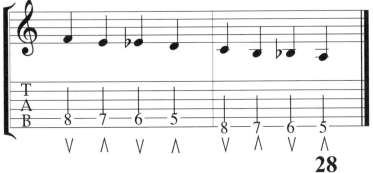

Practice Exercises 25 & 26 along with the G scale for at least 5 minutes each day. You will notice a significant improvement in both right and left hand coordination within the first three weeks.

It is time to stop and take a quick inventory of where we are. You should have accomplished the following:

1. Mastered the G, C, & D chords and change between them easily.
2. Play an alternating bass rhythm to several songs.
3. Spend 5 minutes a day practicing the G scale and down up picking exercises.
4. If you are proficient at the first three, you will be able to play basic rhythm to many songs.

Review each of the above to be sure that you thoroughly understand them. If you have any questions, we recommend that you either talk to your teacher or review the CD or DVD.

Most students find the following products useful as they progress through the remainder of this course.

The *Acoustic Guitar Practice CDs* is a two CD set that plays the first 18 songs in the *Acoustic Guitar Primer* at three speeds along with an acoustic band (guitar, bass, mandolin, and vocals). All of the verses are sung on each speed with harmony parts where appropriate. Quickly develop the ability to jam with others. 2 CD Set $14.95

The follow up course, *Acoustic Guitar Book 2,* takes you to the next level of playing rhythm guitar by teaching a variety of rock & country strums, arpeggios, bar chords, and how to play along with other guitarists. The student plays and sings along with a full band on extended versions of 17 popular songs. Book $14.95 DVD $14.95

The lyrics to all of the songs in this book are in the *Bluegrass Fakebook*. It contains lyrics, chord progressions, and melody lines to 150 of the all-time favorite Bluegrass songs, including 50 gospel tunes as well as many "new" bluegrass songs. Printed in large, easy-to-read type with one song per page, this book is excellent for use on stage or in jam sessions, because everyone can read along. Also includes chord charts for the guitar, banjo, and mandolin and a listing of currently available recordings of each song. Now all those obscure verses you can never remember are right at your fingertips. $19.95

Strings should be replaced at least every three months, sometimes sooner.

SECTION II

PLAYING

Advanced Rhythm Techniques

ADVANCED RHYTHM TECHNIQUES

From this point on, we'll be applying the rhythm techniques we've studied to some popular standards. With each new song, we will add new strums, chords, or runs to make your rhythm playing more varied and interesting. At the same time, continue spending at least 5 minutes a day on single string exercises (pages 16, 17 and 28).

You should note that each song can be played as simply or as fancy as desired. The techniques learned towards the end of the book can be used on the first songs and likewise, the last songs can be played with the simpler strums we learned earlier. A good bluegrass or country rhythm player uses the basic alternating bass pattern about 90% of the time and uses the other techniques covered in this section to add variety to the rhythm. When and where we deviate from the alternating bass pattern determines our individual sound or style.

EXERCISE 27

We'll add the G7 chord on the next song. Practice the following exercise:

G - G7 - C - G - G7 - C - G - G7 - C

EXERCISE 28

We're going to add a third bass note to the G chord to give it more variety. Practice this before moving to the next song.

31

ROLL IN MY SWEET BABY'S...

Traditional

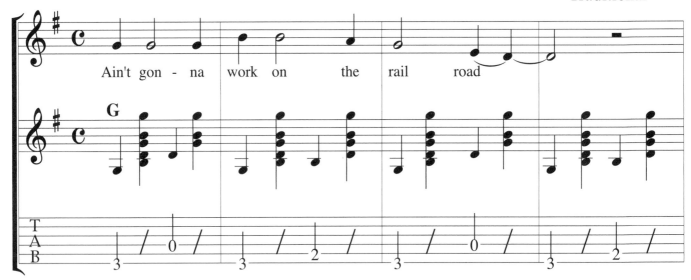

Ain't gon - na work on the rail road

Ain't gon - na work on the farm Gon - na

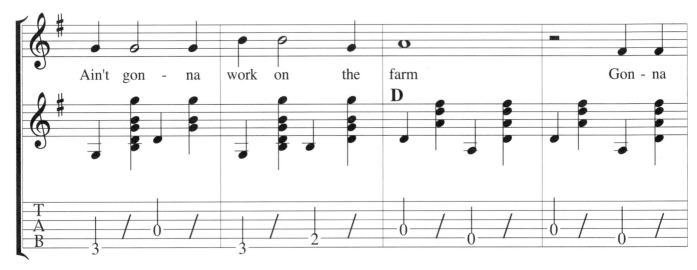

lay round this shack till the mail train comes back And

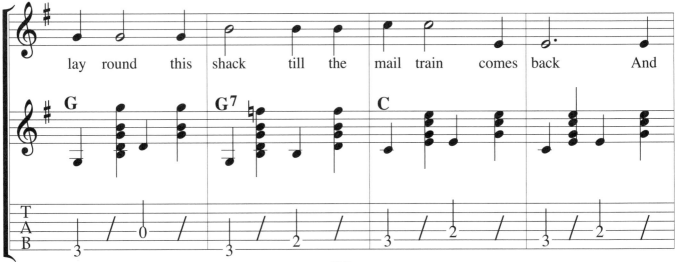

Flatt & Scruggs - The Best of Flatt & Scruggs
Willie Nelson - Willie & Family Live
Nitty Gritty Dirt Band - Will The Circle Be Unbroken Vol III

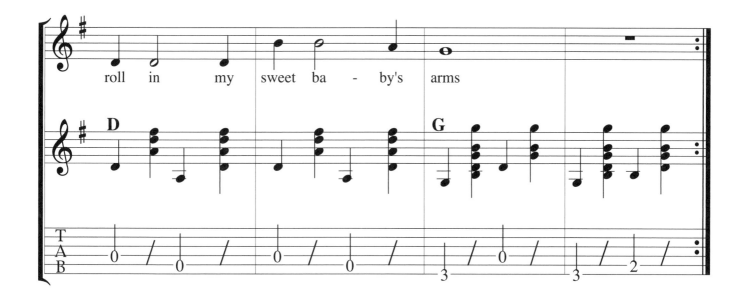

roll in my sweet ba - by's arms

Chorus

Roll in my sweet baby's arms
Roll in my sweet baby's arms
Gonna lay around this shack till the mail train comes back
And roll in my sweet baby's arms

Where were you last Saturday night
While I was laying down in jail
You were out on the street with another man
Wouldn't even try to go my bail

Chorus

Your Mama was a beauty operator
Sister could weave and spin
Daddy owned a piece of that old cotton gin
Watch that money roll in

Chorus

Note - Most of the songs on the CD or DVD will be played at two speeds, slow for practicing and uptempo for performing. There will be a track number for each version on the CD or DVD so that you can practice it over and over.

The *Let's Jam! CD Country & Bluegrass* contains 7 of the songs in this book, extended versions played at 2 speeds. Check with your local music store.

DOWN UP STRUM

Another popular rhythm technique uses a down up strum in place of the down strum. The down up strum takes the same amount of time as the down strum even though the right hand moves twice as far. When using the down up strum, the down stroke is the same as you have been playing, the up stroke is shorter because you only hit the first 3 strings. The following pictures illustrate the up stroke.

Start of Up Stroke

End of Up Stroke

EXERCISE 29

Count 1 2 & 3 4 & out loud. The bass notes will be played on 1 and 3 while the down up strum is played on 2 & and 4 & as follows:

Strum Up

EXERCISE 30

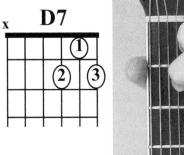

D7

Practice the D7 chord with the following changes:

D - D7 - G - D - D7 - G - D - D7 - G - D - D7 - G

BANKS OF THE OHIO

Joan Baez - Volume 2
Olivia Newton John - The Definitive Collection
Doc Watson/Earl Scruggs/Ricky Skaggs - The Three Pickers

35

EXERCISE 31

40

The 1st joint of the left index finger bars both the 1st and 2nd strings at the 1st fret.

Practice the following chords:

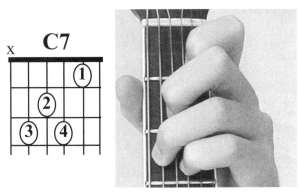

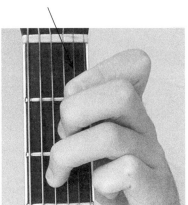

C - F - C - F - C - F - C - F

C - C7 - F - C - C7 - F - C - C7 - F - C - C7 - F

DARK HOLLOW

41-42

Traditional

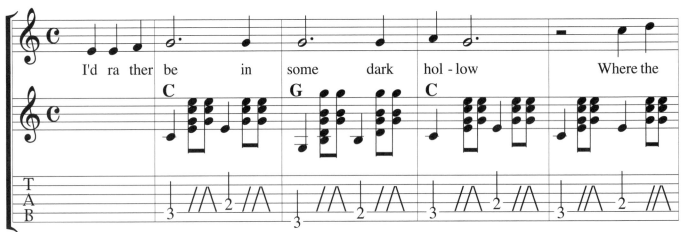

I'd ra ther be in some dark hol - low Where the

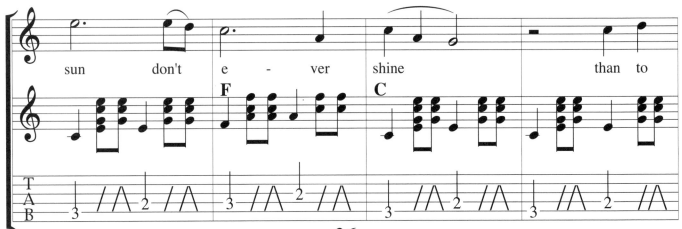

sun don't e - ver shine than to

Chorus

So blow your whistle freight train
Carry me further on down the track
I'm going away, I'm leaving today
I'm going, but I ain't coming back

I'd rather be in some dark hollow
Where the sun don't ever shine
Than to be in some big city
In a small room with your love on my mind

Chorus

Note - At this point, you should start practicing the scale exercises on page 68
for at least 5 - 10 minutes per day.

3/4 TIME

Quite a few bluegrass, folk, & country tunes are played in 3/4 or waltz tempo.
This means there are three beats per measure and it's counted 1 2 & 3 & 1 2 & 3 &.

Bass	Down	Up	Down	Up	Bass	Down	Up	Down	Up
1	2	&	3	&	1	2	&	3	&

EXERCISE 32

IN THE PINES

Traditional

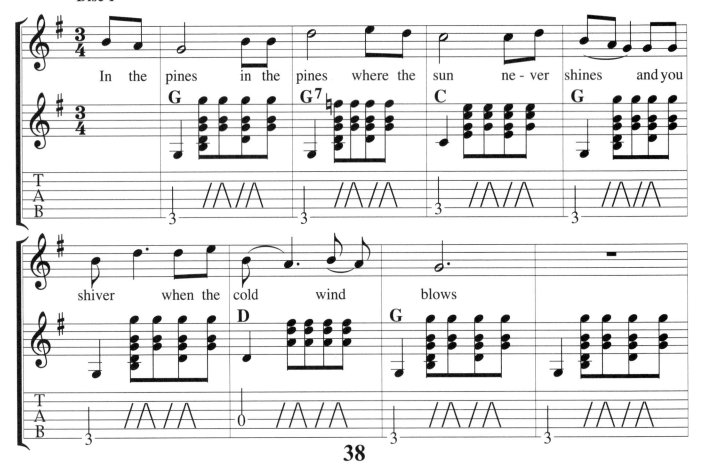

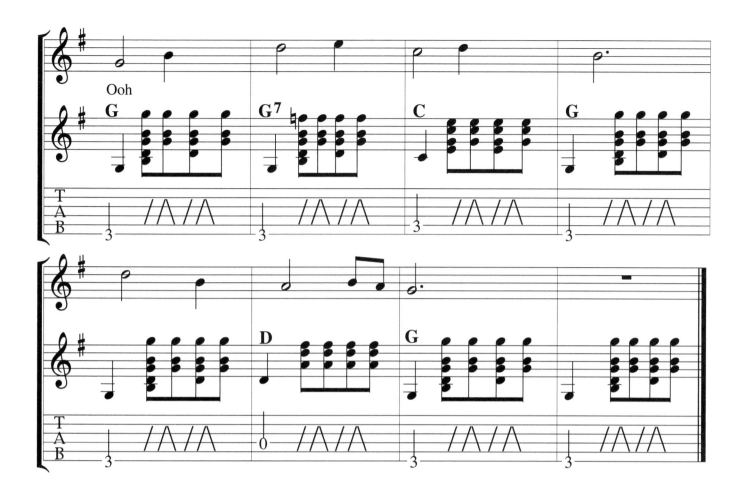

The longest train I ever saw
Went down that Georgia Line
The engine passed at six o'clock
And the cab passed by at nine

Chorus

Little girl, little girl, what have I done
That makes you treat me so
You've caused me to weep, you've caused me to mourn
You've caused me to leave my home

Chorus

Dolly Parton - Heartsongs 1994
Grateful Dead - Birth of the Dead
Leadbelly - Where Did You Sleep Last Night?

EXERCISE 33

 41:45   45

Practice these two chords with the following progressions:

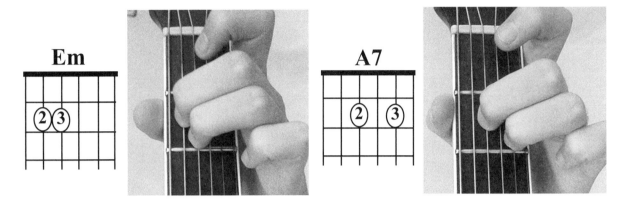

G - Em - D - G - Em - D - G - Em - D

G - A7 - D - G - A7 - D -G - A7 - D

AMAZING GRACE

42:30 46-47

Traditional

40

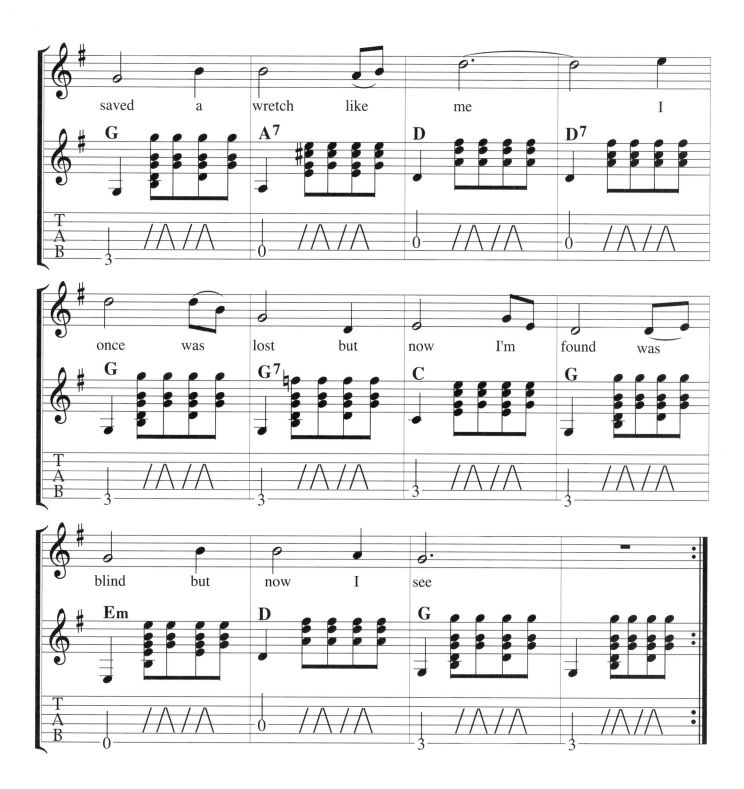

Twas grace that taught my heart to fear
And grace my fears relieved
How precious did that grace appear
The hour I first believed

When we've been here ten thousand years
Bright shining as the sun
We've no less days to sing God's praise
Than when we first begun

Elvis Presley - Amazing Grace: His Sacred Songs
Aretha Franklin - Amazing Grace
Neville Brothers - Live On Planet Earth

41

You should have been practicing the single string technique and be able to play it smoothly by now. If not, go back to Exercises 9 and 10 and review. We'll use these notes out of the G scale as the basis for bass runs to connect the chords together.

Play the following exercise using all down strokes for the bass notes.

 EXERCISE 34

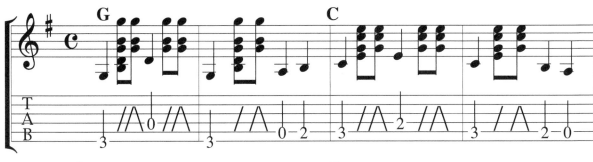

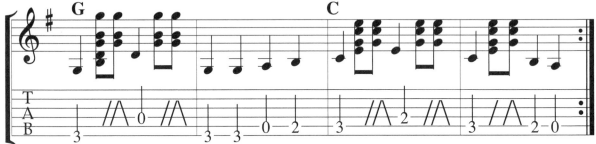

EXERCISE 35

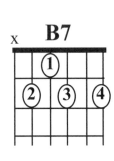 

Practice the B7 chord. The middle finger doesn't move when changing from G to B7.

G - B7 - C - G - B7 - C - G - B7 - C - G - B7 - C

Note - The DVD contains a mistake in the 1st measure of the song. The tablature should read like the 1st measure on the following page.

Bob Dylan - Before the Flood & After The Fire
Lucinda Williams - Ramblin'
Gillian Welch - Soul Journey

EXERCISE 36

Next we'll use a bass run to go from G to D.

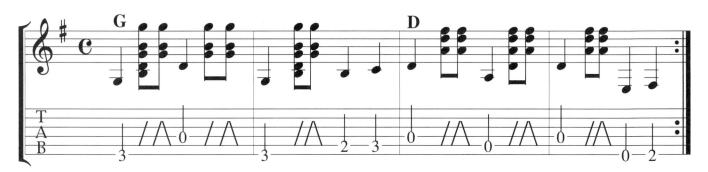

WAY DOWNTOWN

Traditional

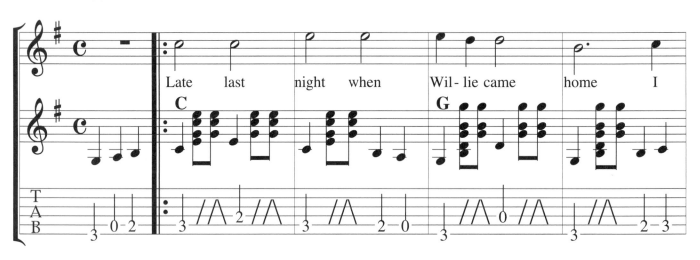

Late   last   night   when   Wil- lie came   home   I

heard   him   rap-ping on   the   door

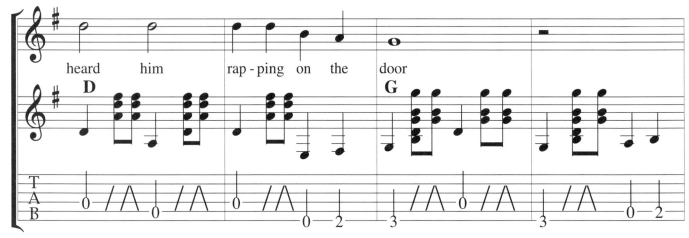

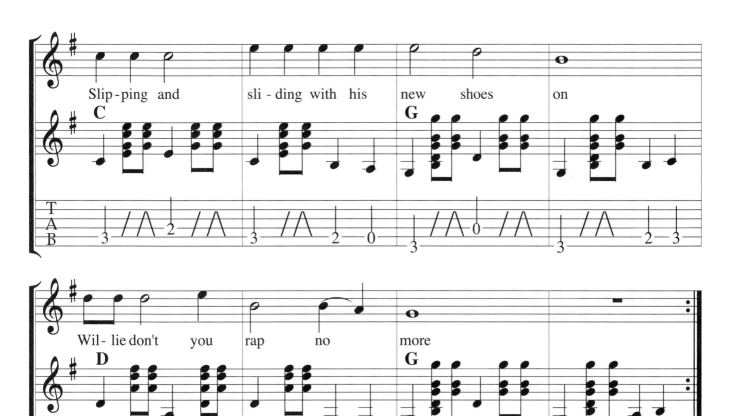

Slip-ping and   sli-ding with his   new   shoes   on

Wil-lie don't   you   rap   no   more

Oh me, oh my
What's gonna become of me
Way downtown, fooling around
Mama, don't you cry for me

One old shirt is all I've got
And a dollar is all I crave
Brought nothing with me into this world
Gonna take nothing to my grave
Chorus

Wish I was down in Old Baltimore
Sitting in an easy chair
One arm around my old guitar
And the other around my dear
Chorus

Wish I had a needle and thread
As fine as I could sew
Sew all the good looking girls to my back
And down the road I'd go
Chorus

Nitty Gritty Dirt Band - Will The Circle Be Unbroken
Doc Watson - The Essential Doc Watson
Tony Rice - Tony Rice

 **EXERCISE 37** 48:20 DVD VIDEO 54

Here's a bass run for G to Em.

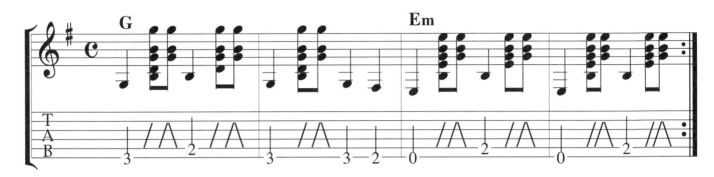

EXERCISE 38

When you have several measures of G in a row, you can give your playing more variety by using this lick. Use the middle finger to fret the 4th string at the 2nd fret.

 CD 42-43 AGJ 7-9 Disc 2 # SITTIN ON TOP OF THE WORLD 49:10 DVD VIDEO 55-56

Traditional

She called me up from El Paso
Said come back Daddy, Lord I miss you so.
Now She's gone and I don't worry
Cause I'm sitting on top of the world.

Ashes to ashes, dust to dust
Show me a woman that a man can trust
Now she's gone and I don't worry
Cause I'm sitting on top of the world

Willie Nelson - Milk Cow blues
Bob Dylan - Good As I Been To You
LeAnn Rimes - The Best of LeAnn Rimes

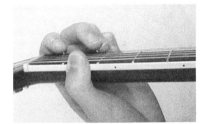
HAMMER ON

A hammer on is a relatively simple technique that will really spice up your playing. It is a two step process.

First Sound - Pick the open 4th string with the right hand while holding a partial G chord. The middle finger is poised above the 4th string 2nd fret, ready to pounce down on it.

Second Sound - Hammer down on the 4th string 2nd fret with the left middle finger to produce a second sound. The right hand does not move. You must move forcefully with a lot of pressure to produce the second note. It will take several attempts to perfect the hammer on.

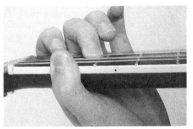

EXERCISE 39

Pick the 4th string as shown. Hammer down on the 4th string 2nd fret to produce a second sound. Do this for two minutes each day until it becomes natural.

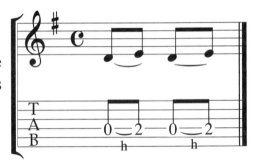

EXERCISE 40

Form a G chord and practice this hammer on. The little and ring fingers remain stationary in the G chord position. The middle finger moves for the hammer ons on the 4th and 5th strings.

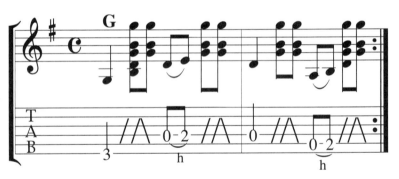

EXERCISE 41

Now practice the hammer on with the C chord. The ring and index fingers remain stationary while the middle finger is used for the hammer on.

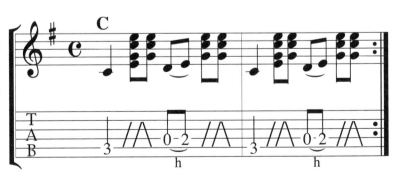

WABASH CANNONBALL

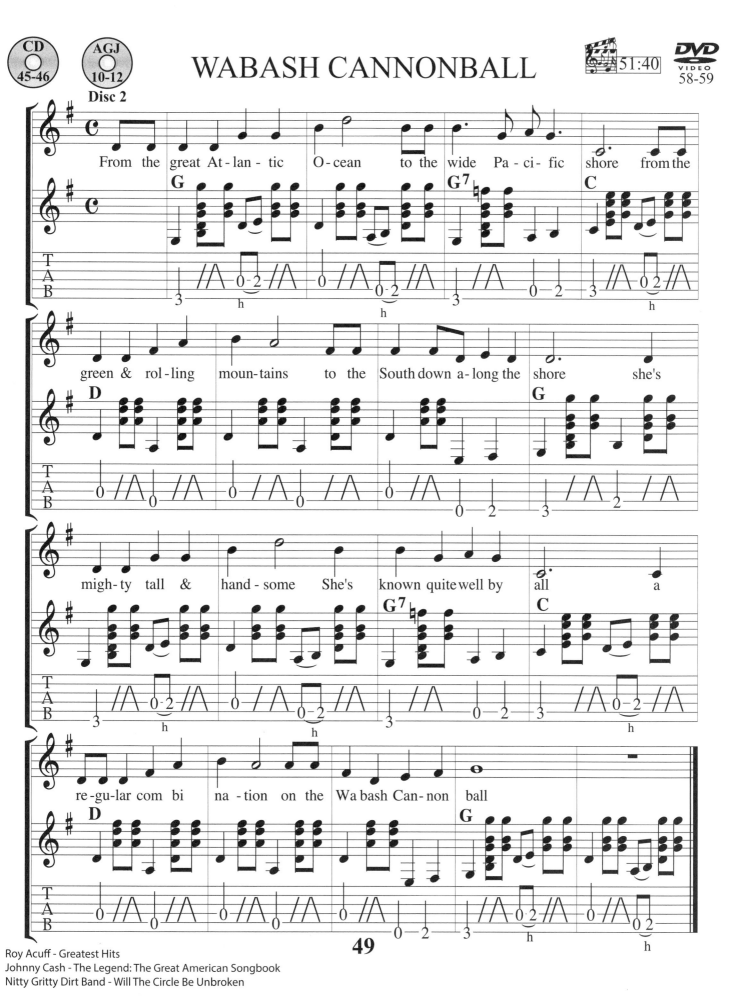

EXERCISE 42

This is a G run that will be used at the end of a musical phrase for accent.

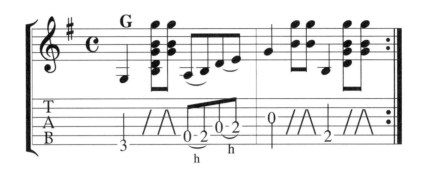

EXERCISE 43

Here's a new walk from G to D.

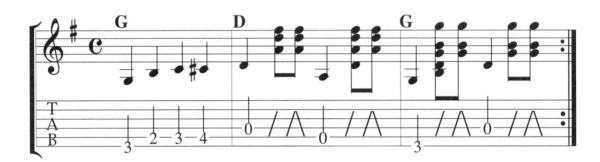

Practice these two exercises until you are comfortable with them, then we'll use them in the next song.

Note - *Crying Holy* is the last song on the DVD. The rest of the material in the book will be on the CD. Make sure to listen to the CD as you practice the remaining exercises and songs.

Traditional

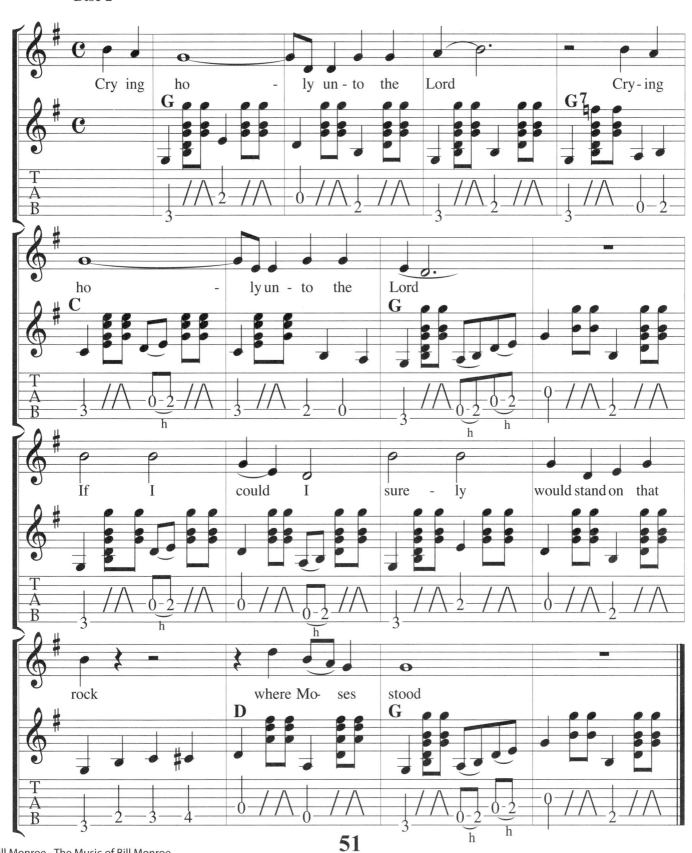

Next we'll play the rhythm to a couple of
popular bluegrass fiddle tunes that have some
interesting chord progressions. In measure 3, use
the following fingering for the F chord:

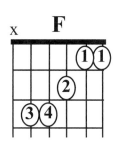

SALT RIVER

Traditional

Doc Watson - On Stage
Nickel Creek - Random Songs
Norman Blake - Whiskey Before Breakfast

Next we'll go to the key of C to play rhythm to another fiddle tune. Pay attention to the repeat signs.

BILLY IN THE LOWGROUND

Traditional

Flatt & Scruggs - Live At The Ash Grove
David Grisman - Here Today
Tony Rice - California Autumn

53

THE G RUN

The G run is used quite often in bluegrass to accent the end of a phrase, verse, or chorus. It is also used to start and end instrumental lead guitar breaks. Here are variations of the G run that can be used interchangeably.

Basic G Run

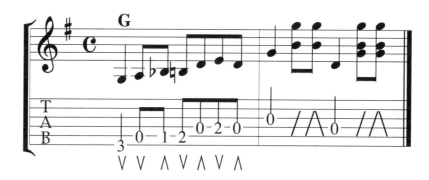

Rhythmic Variation

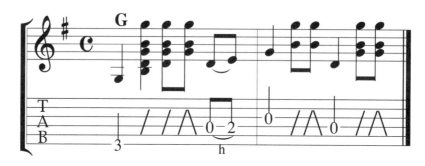

Chromatic Variation

Quarter Note Variation

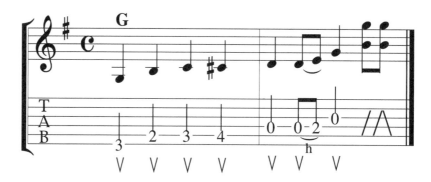

PULL OFFS

Pull offs are the opposite of hammer ons and help add variety to your playing.

EXERCISE 44

First Sound - Pick the 4th string at the 2nd fret to produce the first sound.

Second Sound - While the note is ringing, pull the 2nd finger down and off the string to produce the second sound. It is written like this:

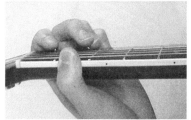

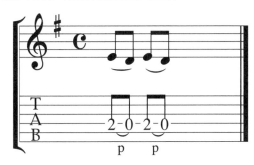

EXERCISE 45

Pull offs can be used in the G run.

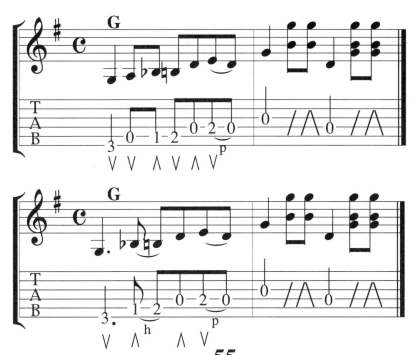

LITTLE MAGGIE

CD 54-55

AGJ 22-24
Disc 2

Traditional

Yon - der stands lit - tle Mag - gie with a dram glass in her hand She's pas - sing a - way her trou - bles by

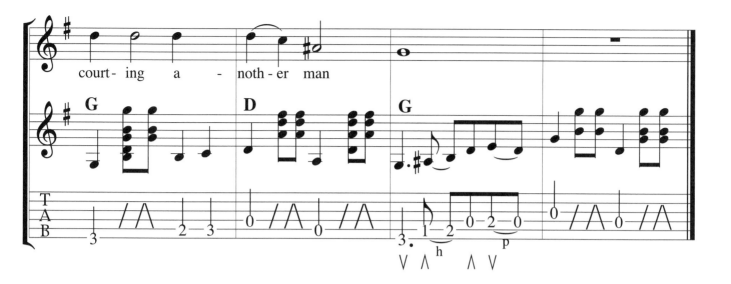

court - ing a - noth - er man

Oh, how can I ever stand it
Just to see them two blue eyes
Shining in the moonlight
Like two diamonds in the skies

Pretty flowers were made for blooming
Pretty stars were made to shine
Pretty women were made for loving
Little Maggie was made for mine

Last time I saw little Maggie
She was setting on the banks of the sea
With a forty four around her
And a banjo on her knee

Lay down your last gold dollar
Lay down your gold watch and chain
Little Maggie's gonna dance for Daddy
Listen to this old banjo ring

Go away, go away little Maggie
Go and do the best you can
I'll get me another woman
You can get you another man

EXERCISE 46

We will use some rhythmic variations for the next song.

EXERCISE 47

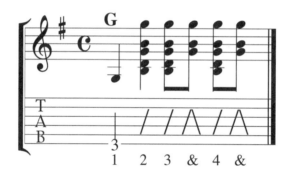

NINE POUND HAMMER

Traditional

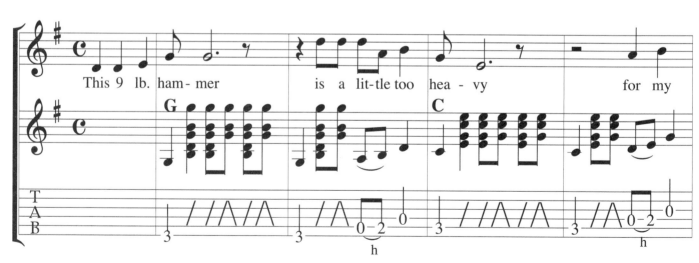

John Prine - Sweet Revenge
Jerry Garcia & David Grisman - Been All Around This World
Johnny Cash - Blood, Sweat, & Tears

59

SECTION III
LEAD PLAYING

Section III will deal with playing lead guitar (flatpicking). There are two basic approaches to bluegrass lead playing:

1. **Chord Style** - This involves using the basic rhythm techniques we have been studying and picking out the melody on the bass notes.

2. **Single String Style** - This is similar to playing scales and scale exercises. The melody is played with single notes using down up picking.

SLIDES

A slide is a technique similar to a hammer on and is played as follows:

First Sound - Play the 3rd string noted at the 2nd fret. The middle finger of the left hand is used to note the 3rd string.

Second Sound - While the note is ringing, slide your middle finger up to the 3rd string 4th fret. The middle finger presses down on the 3rd string as it travels from the 2nd fret to the 4th fret.

Practice the following exercise until you can play it clearly.

EXERCISE 48

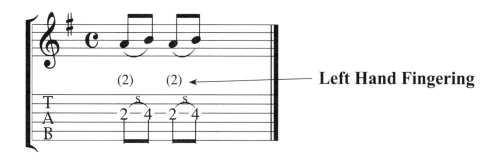

WILDWOOD FLOWER CHORDS

In *Wildwood Flower*, we will using the following fingering to go from G to the C chord. Note that the ring finger and little finger remain in place as you switch from one to the other.

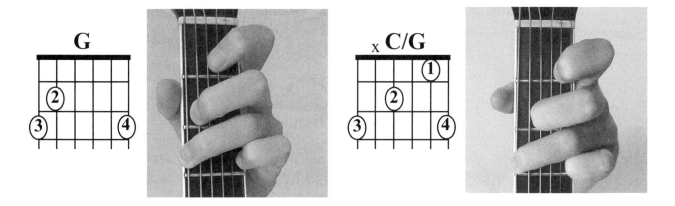

JOHN HARDY CHORDS

John Hardy on page 64 uses these fingerings for the C chord in measures 2 and 3.

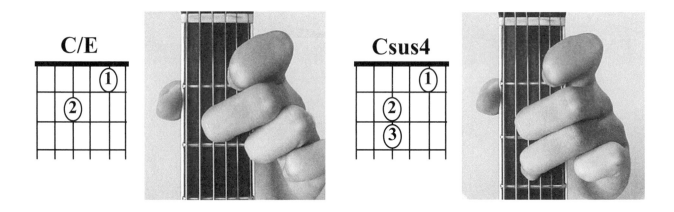

Note - Before attempting the songs on the following pages, you should practice the scale exercises on page 68 and Exercises 25 and 26 on page 28 to strengthen your left hand and to improve the accuracy of your right hand.

WILDWOOD FLOWER

Traditional

Carter Family - Wildwood Flower
Emmylou Harris - The Ballad Of Sally Rose
Johnny Cash - Live At Madison Square Gardens

JOHN HARDY

Traditional

George Thorogood - Box Of The Blues
Leadbelly - Goodnight Irene
Tony Rice - Cold On The Shoulder

The next songs will utilize the scale exercises on page 68. Make sure you are comfortable with these exercises before attempting these songs.

OLD JOE CLARK

Traditional

John Hartford - Morning Bugle
Hank Williams - Health & Happiness Shows
Chet Atkins & Doc Watson - Reflections

65

BLACKBERRY BLOSSOM

Traditional

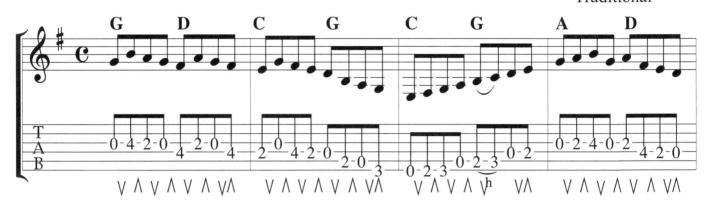

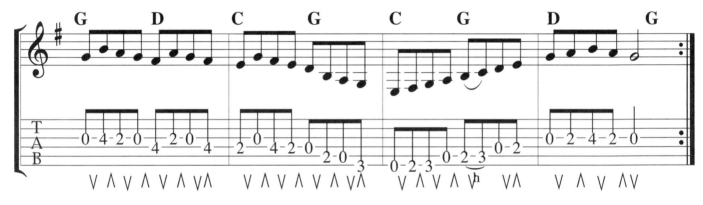

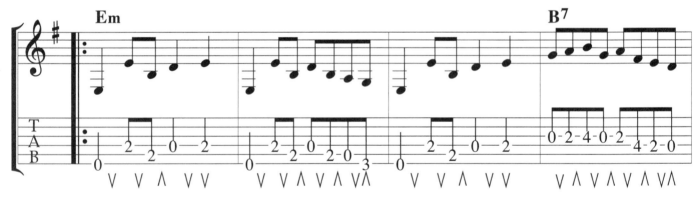

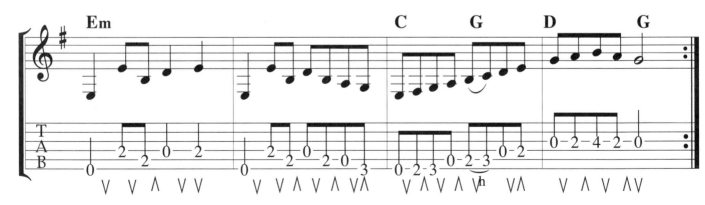

Tony Rice - Manzanita
Doc Watson - The Essential Doc Watson
John Hartford - The Speed Of The Old Long Bow

WILL THE CIRCLE BE UNBROKEN

Traditional

Nitty Gritty Dirt Band - Will The Circle Be Unbroken
Willie Nelson - Willie & Family Live
Gregg Allman - Laid Back

SCALE EXERCISES

EXERCISE 48

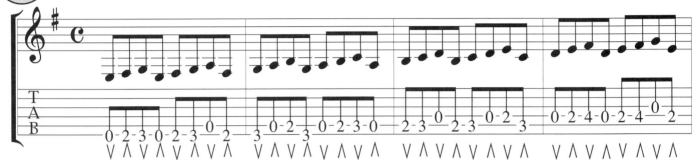

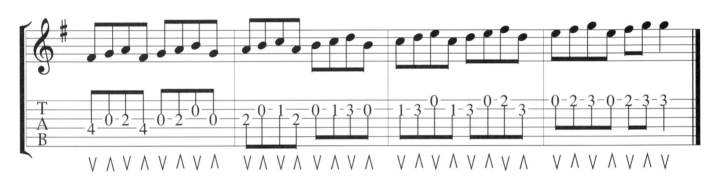

EXERCISE 49

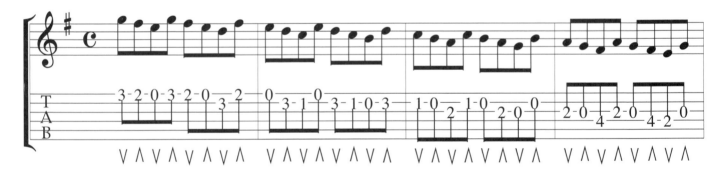

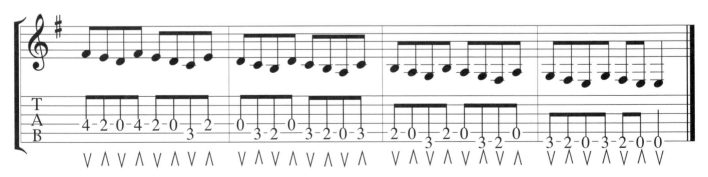

68

MUSIC THEORY

To become an accomplished guitarist you must understand some basic principals about the guitar and music in general so that you can get the overall picture of the music you are playing.

A major scale consists of 7 notes, which we will number 1-7.

Notes In Major Scales

Scale		1	2	3	4	5	6	7
Key of C		C	D	E	F	G	A	B
Key of G	(1#)	G	A	B	C	D	E	F#
Key of D	(2#)	D	E	F#	G	A	B	C#
Key of A	(3#)	A	B	C#	D	E	F#	G#
Key of E	(4#)	E	F#	G#	A	B	C#	D#
Key of F	(1b)	F	G	A	Bb	C	D	E
Key of Bb	(2b)	Bb	C	D	Eb	F	G	A
Key of Eb	(3b)	Eb	F	G	Ab	Bb	C	D
Key of Ab	(4b)	Ab	Bb	C	Db	Eb	F	G

A **chromatic scale** consists of 12 notes, all the notes possible to play in one octave. All of the notes are shown below. The notes on top of each other are identical. For instance, the A# and the Bb are the same. These are called **enharmonic tones**.

Chromatic Scale

1	2	3	4	5	6	7	8	9	10	11	12
A	A#	B	C	C#	D	D#	E	F	F#	G	G#
	Bb			Db		Eb			Gb		Ab

Notice that there is no note between B & C, and no note between E & F. A **half step** is one note in the chromatic scale (A to A# is a half step). This corresponds to one fret on the guitar. A **whole step** is two notes in the chromatic scale (A to B is a whole step). This corresponds to two frets on the guitar.

To figure out the notes in any major scale, use the following guides:

Notes	1	2	3	4	5	6	7	1
	whole step	whole step	half step	whole step	whole step	whole step	half step	

For example, to figure out the notes in an A scale, start with an A note in the chromatic scale. To go to note 2 make a whole step to B (2 frets on the guitar). Note 3 would be a whole step to C#. Note 4 is a half step to D (1 fret on the guitar). Note 5 is a whole step to E. Note 6 is a whole step to F#. Note 7 is a whole step to G#. Note 1 is a half step back to A.

A relationship exists between scales and chords known as **chord progressions**. We started with several three chord songs. The most common chords used are the 1st, 4th, & 5th chords of a key. For example, we first played in the key of G, using the G, C, & D chords. There are many songs that use only these three chords.

The following chart shows the common chord progressions that you will encounter:

Common Chords		Commonly Called	Example
1st	1st note of scale (major chord)	(Tonic) G	
4th	4th note of scale (major chord)	(Subdominant)	C
5th	5th note of scale (major chord)	(Dominant)	D
6th minor	6th note of scale (minor chord)	(Relative Minor)	Em
2nd	2nd note of scale (major chord)		A
2nd minor	2nd note of scale (minor chord)		Am
3rd	3rd note of scale (major chord)		B
3rd minor	3rd note of scale (minor chord)		Bm
b7th	7th note of scale moved down a half step (major chord)		F
1 (7th)	1st note of scale (dominant 7th chord) 1→ 1 (7th) → 4		G7
5 (7th)	5th note of scale (dominant 7th chord) 5→ 5 (7th)→ 1		D7
b3rd	3rd note of scale moved down a half step (major chord)		Bb
b6th	6th note of scale moved down a half step (major chord)		Eb

A **major chord** consists of three notes, the 1st, 3rd, & 5th notes of that particular scale. Although we are often strumming 6 strings at a time, we are only playing a combination of three notes. For example, the first chord we played was a G chord, which consists of G, B, & D. The 6 notes played when you strum an open G chord are G, B, D, G, B, & G.

A **dominant 7th chord**, commonly called the 7th chord, is a four note chord consisting of the 1st, 3rd, 5th, & b7th notes of that scale. The 7th sound comes from adding the b7th note (7th lowered a half step). For example, a G7 chord is composed of G, B, D, & F.

A **minor chord** consists of three notes, the 1st, b3rd, & 5th notes of that scale. The minor sound comes from lowering the 3rd a half step. A Gm chord is composed of G, Bb, & D.

A **minor 7th chord** consists of the 1st, b3rd, 5th, & b7th notes of that scale. For example, a Gm7 is composed of G, Bb, D, & F.

The following chart shows what notes these and other common chords are composed of:

Chord	Notes	Example	
Major	1st, 3rd, 5th	G	G, B, D
7th	1st, 3rd, 5th, b7th	G7	G, B, D, F
Minor	1st, b3rd, 5th	Gm	G, Bb, D
Minor 7th	1st, b3rd, 5th, b7th	Gm7	G, Bb, D, F
Major 7th	1st, 3rd, 5th, 7th	Gmaj7	G, B, D, F#
9th	1st, 2nd, 3rd, 5th, b7th	G9	G, A, B, D, F
sus4	1st, 3rd, 4th, 5th	Gsus4	G, B, C, D
Diminished	1st, b3rd, b5th, 6th	Gdim	G, Bb, Db, E
Augmented	1st, 3rd, #5th	G+	G, B, D#

CIRCLE OF 5THS

The circle of 5ths is useful for memorizing the order of sharp or flat keys, as well as the order in which the sharps or flats occur.

Beginning with the key of C and moving clockwise in steps of 5ths, each key has one more sharp than the one before it. Moving counterclockwise from C in steps of 4ths, each key has one more flat than the one before it.

Each new sharp is the 7th of the key in which it occurs. Each new flat is the 4th of the key in which it occurs.

The key signatures as they would appear in music notation are shown inside the circle. To figure out the name of the flat keys from the key signature, use the next to last flat. Move the last sharp up one note (1/2 step or 1 fret) to figure out the name of the sharp keys.

Notice that there are 12 different major keys, but three of them have different names. Keys that have the same key signature, but have different names are called enharmonic keys.

The relative minor key of each major key, which is the 6th of that key, is shown inside the circle. The relative minor has the same key signature as its relative major key.

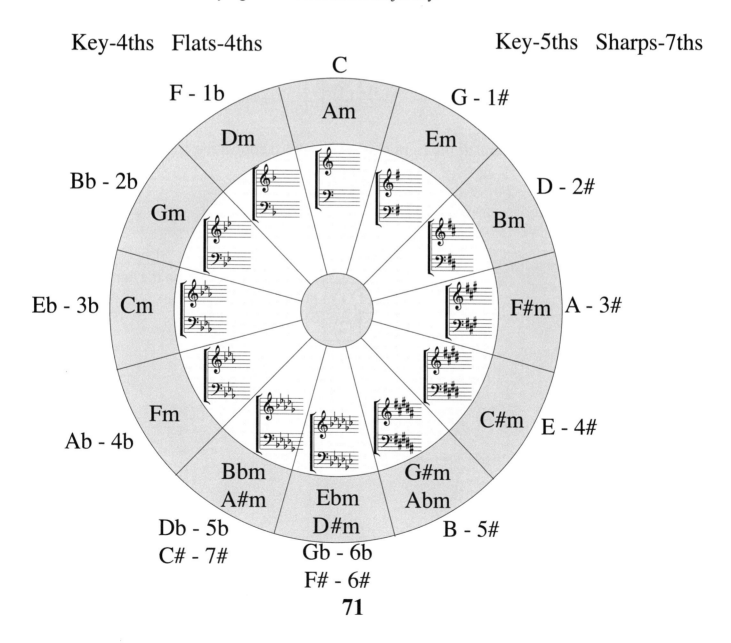

71

CHORD CHART

There is a chord chart on the following page that shows all of the common chords you will encounter. Notice that they are laid out in sequence with all of the different type chords on the same line. For instance, all of the different G chords are on the first line. They are also aligned vertically in finger patterns. For example, all of the 7th chords are in the third column.

The small x on top of the chord diagram means don't strum this string because it would be a note that is not in the chord.

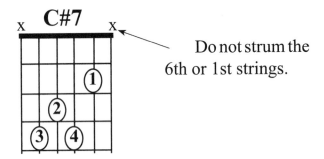

Do not strum the 6th or 1st strings.

The Roman numeral at the right side of the chord shows the fret position of the index finger.

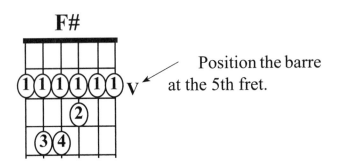

Position the barre at the 5th fret.

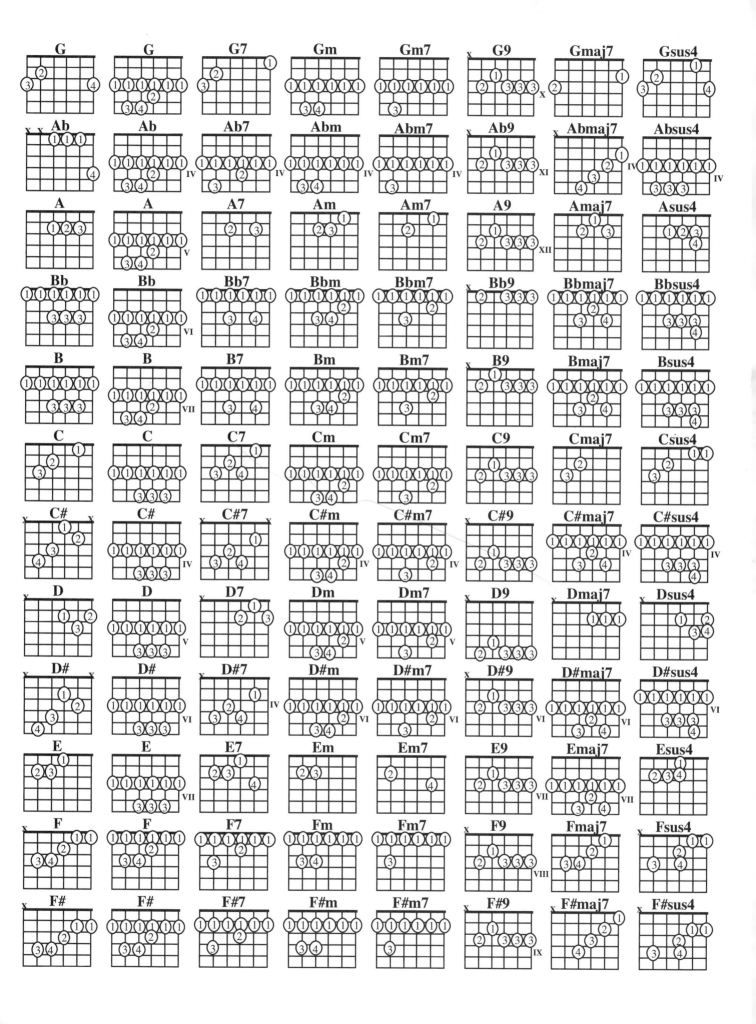

WHAT TO DO NEXT

Taking private lessons from a qualified teacher is always a good idea. Check with your local music store to find a good instructor.

Companion DVD To *Acoustic Guitar Primer*

The *Intro to Acoustic Guitar DVD* allows you to see all the movements of the left and right hand. It covers the material in the book utilizing the latest in video technology (split screen, on screen tablature, state of the art graphics, special effects, and animation) to add further emphasis and clarity for the student. DVD $9.95

Practice CDs for *Acoustic Guitar Primer*

The *Acoustic Guitar Practice CDs* is a two CD set that plays the first 18 songs in the *Acoustic Guitar Primer* at three speeds along with an acoustic band (guitar, bass, mandolin, and vocals). All of the verses are sung on each speed with harmony parts where appropriate. Quickly develop the ability to jam with others. 2 CD Set $14.95

Play 17 Popular Songs With A Full Band

The follow up course, *Acoustic Guitar Book 2,* takes you to the next level of playing rhythm guitar by teaching a variety of rock & country strums, arpeggios, bar chords, and how to play along with other guitarists. The student plays and sings along with a full band on extended versions of 17 popular songs.

Book $14.95 DVD $14.95

Play Bluegrass Lead Guitar

If you want to continue with bluegrass lead guitar, *Flatpicking Guitar Songs* book with CD teaches how to become a flatpicker. Includes exciting arrangements to popular songs and is written in both tablature and notation. There are several breaks for each song and each break is played slow (for practicing) and fast (for performing) on the audio CD.

Book $14.95

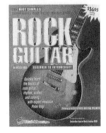

Play Rock & Roll On The Acoustic Guitar

If you're interested in rock & roll, *Introduction to Electric Guitar DVD* and *Electric Guitar Primer* book with CD teach the basics of rock & roll rhythm and also work fine with an acoustic guitar. It teaches rock & roll riffs, power chords, chords & strumming, and scales. The student plays along with a full band.

Book $15.95 DVD $9.95

Followup To The Electric Guitar Course

Introduction to Rock Guitar DVD and *Rock Guitar Book* with CD is the follow-up to the Electric Guitar course and teaches more advanced rhythm techniques and lead playing using the minor pentatonic scales. It shows all the techniques that legendary rock guitarists use to get those famous sounds. It also contains a hot licks section.

Book $14.95 DVD $14.95

To find these courses, contact your local music store or contact the number and address on the back cover of this book. You can also look up our web site at cvls.com.